Prayers

For

SUCCESSFUL

Real Estate

Professionals

Table of Contents

To be a truly Successful Real Estate Professional, you must play by the rules... God's Rules.

"Trust the Lord with all your heart, and don't depend on your own understanding. Remember the Lord in all you do, and he will give you success." Proverbs 3:5-6 NCV

Starting in the Real Estate Industry

BUILD YOUR FOUNDATION ON A SOLID ROCK

"Everyone then who hears these words of mine and does them will be like a wise man who built his house on the rock. And the rain fell, and the floods came, and the winds blew and beat on that house, but it did not fall, because it had been founded on the rock. And everyone who hears these words of mine and does not do them will be like a foolish man who built his house on the sand. And the rain fell, and the floods came, and the winds blew and beat against that house, and it fell, and great was the fall of it." - Matthew 7:24-27

Let Us Pray...

Father God, I ask for your help in starting my own business. You are my strongest ally, and my best partner. Please join me in this new venture so that I may succeed for myself, my family and the customers I will serve. Grant me your powers of good judgment, your wisdom and guidance, so that my business may prosper and do right by us all. God grant me the inspiration, the motivation, the right direction, and the resources to succeed in my new business. My intent is clear, and my will is strong. Help me stay focused on my goals and to reap honest rewards for the benefit of all. Thank You, God for your kind assistance. In Jesus Name Amen.

LET US

PRAY!

Prayer Is So Important And Powerful

"Do not be anxious about anything, but in every situation, by prayer and petition, with thanksgiving, present your requests to God."
Philippians 4:6

For followers of Jesus Christ, prayer is the best way to communicate with God. Prayer is one of the most important things a Christian can do. It is a time where we are communicating with God, and it should be taken very seriously. While there is deep theological meaning in prayer, it doesn't have to be something that is complicated and difficult. It's something anyone can do anywhere at any time.

> *Psalm 5:3, "In the morning, O LORD, you hear my voice; in the morning, I lay my requests before you and wait in expectation."*

Prayer is the vehicle for daily dialog with the One who created us. The importance of daily communication through prayer cannot be overestimated. It is so important that it is mentioned over 250 times in Scripture. So why is daily prayer so important? Daily prayer gives us an opportunity to share all aspects of our lives with God. Daily prayer gives us the chance to express our gratitude for the things He provides. Daily prayer provides the platform for confessing our sin and asking for help in overcoming that sin. Daily prayer is an act of worship and obedience, and daily prayer is a way to acknowledge who is really in control of our lives.

1 Thessalonians 5:17,
"Pray without ceasing."

Prayer Brings Light to Darkness

Sometimes we forget just how powerful prayer is. We aren't fighting against something imaginary. Our prayers are fighting against spiritual battles that linger in dark places. Ephesians 6:12 says, "For our struggle is not against flesh and blood, but against the rulers, against the authorities, against the powers of this dark world and against the spiritual forces of evil in the heavenly realms." The power of prayer is so great; it has the power to defeat the devil and his power over us. He wants to destroy us, but God wants to bring us closer to Him. Prayer is our tool to win that battle. Prayer gives us the strength and the faith to finish the race victorious.

> *"But when you pray, go into your room and shut the door and pray to your Father who is in secret. And your Father who sees in secret will reward you."*
>
> *Matthew 6:6*

Drawing Near to God

It's impossible to know someone if you don't spend time with them. Prayer is an opportunity to spend time with God. To really understand the heart of God, you need to pray. In John 15:15 Jesus says: "He no longer calls us his servants, but calls us His friends." Talking with God develops a deeper relationship with Him. The deeper the relationship becomes, the more time you want to spend with Him. In 1 Corinthians 3:9, God calls us His fellow workers. How can we be His fellow workers if we refuse to talk to Him?

> *"Call to me and I will answer you, and will tell you great and hidden things that you have not known."*
>
> *Jeremiah 33:3*

Prayer Protects

Protection is yours just for the asking. You need to pray for protection for your loved ones every day. Pray for loved ones by name, one by one. You can never pray too much for one person. Sometimes it helps to make a list of all the people that you need to pray for each day. Doing this not only offers protection, but also sets a great example for your children.

> " *First of all, then, I urge that supplications, prayers, intercessions, and thanksgivings be made for all people, for kings and all who are in high positions, that we may lead a peaceful and quiet life, godly and dignified in every way. This is good, and it is pleasing in the sight of God our Savior, who desires all people to be saved and to come to the knowledge of the truth.*"
>
> *1 Timothy 2:1-4*

Prayer Changes Us

You often think prayer changes God. This simply isn't the case. Prayer changes you. When you spend time with God, He is working to change your heart to be more like His. The more time you spend with Him, the more you are like Him. Your habits and lifestyles change. You no longer live a self-centered life, but one that is focused on others with a pure and sincere heart. Prayer changes you inside out.

> *Pray then like this: "Our Father in heaven, hallowed be your name. Your kingdom come, your will be done, on earth as it is in heaven. Give us this day our daily bread, and forgive us our debts, as we also have forgiven our debtors. And lead us not into temptation, but deliver us from evil."*
>
> *Matthew 6:9-13*

Prayer Brings Breakthroughs in Life

One of the most important aspects of prayer in your life are the breakthroughs. Sometimes you are faced with devastating circumstances and feel you have nowhere to turn. It's at that point we should pray (although there should have plenty of prayer beforehand, too). Fasting and praying are powerful too. Sometimes you need a message from God, and you need to be solely focused on Him to get it. It may be painful during the prayer and waiting process but once you receive it, you will be so happy you sought Him. While you wait, you can also sing praise songs, read the Bible, or do anything else that brings you closer to Him. Even if the breakthrough doesn't happen that day, you will receive the strength and the grace to carry on. Eventually, you will receive an answer to your prayers or a peace about waiting longer. When you look back over this time, you will most likely see it as the most spiritually rich time of your life.

> *Psalm 34:17, "When the righteous cry for help, the Lord hears and delivers them out of all their troubles."*

Dear Lord, make me a person of constant prayer. Your Holy Word commands me to pray without ceasing. In all things great and small, at all times, whether happy or sad, let me seek Your wisdom and Your strength…
In Jesus Name Amen.

Prayers Of The Righteous

"The effectual fervent prayer of a righteous man availeth much." James 5:16

LET US PRAY...

Heavenly Father, please guide me in becoming more prosperous, every day in every way. As I awaken with the gift of yet another day and prepare for the tasks at hand, I offer up this most ardent prayer:

God your blessings make me worthy and deserving of everything that I want in my life.

I pray I will always be in a job that supplies others shelter because people always need homes.

I pray for the wisdom to expect abundance in my life that it surrounds me and is available for the taking and to be shameless and unapologetic upon its receipt, for I deserve abundance.

I pray for a cheerful countenance be it clear or cloudy skies and that I may radiate and affect others with my positive attitude.

I believe and trust in you my God with my own eventual success.

I pray for the trust of others that they may recognize my sincerity and true intentions so that we may move forward together.

I pray for continued clarity of purpose so that I may hold my vision steady and keep my focus on the needs and success of others which in turn shall bring me my success.

I pray for the strength to fend off adversity and use my desire and determination as both weapon and shield.

I pray for the courage to carry forth my convictions during the battle of business and to resist temptation to gain a quicker monetary result. I pray for the strength to combat temptation that compromises those things for which I stand.

I pray that I may be used as a lightning rod to collect the amazing ideas already present in the universe and when blessed with such inspiration, that I may be able to apply my talents and abilities to turn the power of thought into a measurable advancement of my goals.

I pray the love of my work continues to show itself with confidence to my clients.

I pray to retain my childhood wonder so that I can recognize and revel in the small miracles of each day that others may miss.

LET US PRAY...

I pray for an infinite supply of self-confidence for it alone fortifies faith, strengthens my resolve and conquers the largest enemy I will ever face—fear.

I pray for the trust of clients and that makes me rich as a Real Estate Professional.

I pray for a compassionate spirit and the patience to offer those who seek my advice and my help to give them my full and undivided attention.

I pray for good health and a feeling of wellbeing, and the continued desire to improve those areas of my physical life I may be neglecting in the name of my spiritual and entrepreneurial advancement.

I pray that today is a day of excellence and at its conclusion, I am able to acknowledge and to be grateful for the forward motion I have made and the growth I have experienced.

I pray most of all for the understanding and support of those closest to my heart, my family. I pray they will equate what appears like endless hours of apparent pre-occupation with business to what is at the very core of my being, my love for them. For once I achieve what I have set out in its fullest, I will become that more complete being I strive to be.

It is for these things that I pray, for I am Real Estate Professional.

"And if we know that he hears us—whatever we ask—we know that we have what we asked of him." 1 John 5:15

LET US PRAY...

HEAVENLY FATHER, I know I have the dreams of others balanced in my hands and am capable of delivering. I know no client is too difficult for me. Father God, I come into your presence with humility, giving honor and praise to Your Magnificent Name. Thank You for the challenges of my past, Thank You for the power in the present moment and Thank You for the possibilities that await me in my future!

As I look ahead at what the future holds for my Real Estate business, I choose not to worry. You gave me the vision of this business, and I trust that You will give the provision needed for unprecedented success in the coming years.

I make a fortune doing something I enjoy. Right now, in the name of Jesus, I bless each and every day of the upcoming years. I am qualified by experience to give people value for their money.

Lord I know that there is a millionaire on the inside of me and I know that You want me to prosper. I make good money from everything that I do. So over the next 365 days Lord, grant me stamina so that I am able to go the distance and to exceed my client's expectations.

Psalm 112:3, "Wealth and riches are in his house, and his righteousness endures forever."

Thank you for making me motivated and productive. Thank you for clarity so that I can hear the sound of your voice and make my decisions quickly, based on your guidance.

Thank you for focus so that I don't get distracted with nonsense that is outside of your will for my business. Thank you that others see me as someone who persistently strives for success; that is all because of your guidance.

Thank You for boldness, so that I will fearlessly ask for what I want; raise my rates when necessary; say no to clients who don't value me. Thank You for helping me to always remember to come to you in prayer first.

Bless my mind Lord that I might have the courage to think bigger than I ever have before. Let YOUR vision for my business become MY vision for my business.

Thank You Lord for the right money mindset. Thank You that my spirit is open to the level of success you want me to have.

LET US PRAY...

Bless my gifts and talents that I might use them to glorify You!

> *"Furthermore, as for every man to whom God has given riches and wealth, He has also empowered him to eat from them and to receive his reward and rejoice in his labor; this is the gift of God."*

> *Ecclesiastes 5:19*

Thank You Lord for an overflow of clients that no one else can serve like me and thank You Father for an overflow of contracts, cash and opportunities. Thank You for supernatural debt freedom this year. Thank you for blessings wherever I go!

Thank You Lord for the right support team who will help me grow and give me freedom. Thank You for a strong foundation that will help my business weather any storm. Thank You that my family supports my vision. Thank You Lord for powerful and innovative strategies that will propel me to my next divine level.

Thank You for million dollar ideas and the courage to follow through on them.

"But you shall remember the LORD your God, for it is He who is giving you power to make wealth, that He may confirm His covenant which He swore to your fathers, as it is this day." Deuteronomy 8:18

Thank You for divine grace, favor, mercy, access and influence in my industry. Thank You for supernaturally opening doors; thank you for visibility. Thank You for mentors who believe in me. Thank You for the courage to stay on the path that You have laid out for me.

I thank You God of the Heavens that You have blessed me with the opportunity to be in business for myself, and I declare and decree that this year will be a multi-million dollar, debt-free, breakthrough year for God-believing and God-loving Real Estate Professionals around the world.

And so it is! And so it shall be! In Jesus Name Amen.

So Much To Be Grateful For

"A Psalm for giving thanks. Psalm 100:1-5, Make a joyful noise to the Lord, all the earth! Serve the Lord with gladness! Come into his presence with singing! Know that the Lord, he is God! It is he who made us, and we are his; we are his people, and the sheep of his pasture. Enter his gates with thanksgiving, and his courts with praise! Give thanks to him; bless his name! For the Lord is good; his steadfast love endures forever, and his faithfulness to all generations. "

LET US PRAY....

I am grateful for the people who come to me for advice and who trust me.

I am grateful for being able to enjoy architecture at its best.

I am grateful for my customers who give me feedback to build a better company.

I am grateful for my prospects who ask smart questions to make me be better.

I am grateful for being the best Real Estate Professional in the business.

I am grateful for my vendors and partners who help our company do things we couldn't do on our own.

I am grateful for my management team who leads the company through good times and bad.

I am grateful for all of our employees who work hard every day to accomplish our mission.

I am grateful for our advisors and investors who give me the guidance and cash necessary to grow.

I am grateful for the print, broadcast and social media for helping to get the word out about what we do.

I am grateful for my fellow colleagues who teach me through their experiences and insights.

I am grateful for my friends who understand the sacrifices I make with my time.

I am grateful for my family who love me and support me unconditionally.

I am grateful for God for guiding me on the right path.

Today, and every day, I am a grateful Real Estate Industry Professional.

Matthew 6:21

" For where your treasure is, there your heart will be also."

LET US PRAY...

Dear God, by Your grace I am able to win new clients easily. Thank you for granting me the gift of another day to impact people in the way that only I know how. I offer up my gratitude for the unique gifts and talents you have bestowed upon me, that I may be a blessing to the world around me. Thank you that I am able to win new deals by using my expertise. Allow me to always walk in truth and integrity as I present my Real Estate business to the marketplace in a way that is pleasing to you. Surround me with the right people, resources and clients that will lift me up and support the vision you have given me. I decree and declare that word of my Real Estate business will stretch as far as the east is to the west and that thousands of people will be blessed by my hands. Guide me by ordering my footsteps and directing my tongue as I share my passion, knowledge and expertise with the masses. I thank you for prosperity and abundant financial growth in my Real Estate business that I may give back to you. Keep me focused, unshakable and unstoppable in my assignment. And as you continue to make my name great, I will give you all of the glory! In Jesus Name Amen

"And I will make of thee a great nation, and will bless thee, and make thy name great; and thou shalt be a blessing." – Genesis 12:2

Bible Verses That Can Help The Real Estate Professional In You

"Do not toil to acquire wealth; be discerning enough to desist." – Proverbs 23:4

There's nothing inherently wrong with being rich. But there is something wrong with wearing yourself out to get rich.

"Lazy hands make for poverty, but diligent hands bring wealth." – Proverbs 10:4

The Book of Proverbs is filled with all kinds of fantastic observations about life. This one shows how if you slack off, you're going to be met with poverty. If you're wanting to get ahead in business, be diligent. You don't have to absolutely wear yourself out.

"Whatever you do, work heartily, as for the Lord and not for men, knowing that from the Lord you will receive the inheritance as your reward. You are serving the Lord Christ." – Colossians 3:23-24

Imagine working for the perfect boss. Everything they say and do is absolutely perfect. They make the right choices every time. They speak the right words every time. They are right – you guessed it – 100% of the time. That sounds pretty intimidating, doesn't it?

Wouldn't you step up your game if you were working for the perfect boss? Wouldn't you be careful with how you handled their money, their time, and their other resources? Of course, you would! After all, perfection sees all. When you are working for human masters, you know in the back of your minds that there might be room to slack off. But when your working for God, there's no room to cut corners.

Not only will God be pleased with you when he notices the fit and finish you put into your product or service, but most likely your human masters will notice too. Just make sure you care more about what God thinks than what your human masters think. Do that, and your human masters will probably be pleased as well if they are godly people.

"Sluggards do not plow in season; so at harvest time they look but find nothing." – Proverbs 20:4

Here's a lesson for Real Estate Professionals – always be on the lookout for opportunities that lead to a harvest. This verse is probably more about the virtues of having a willingness to work, but it also talks about working in season. With certain seasons come opportunities. If these opportunities are pushed aside, you might find yourself in need but not reaping anything because you didn't work! Remember that the fruit comes after the labor.

"In vain you rise early and stay up late, toiling for food to eat– for he grants sleep to those he loves." – Psalm 127:2

At first glance, this verse seems to be making a general statement that it's good to get your sleep instead of waking up early and going to bed late. While there's certainly value in getting sleep, perhaps it's saying something more. Here's the first verse of the chapter: *"Unless the LORD builds the house, the builders labor in vain. Unless the LORD watches over the city, the guards stand watch in vain." – Psalm 127:1*

It's always good to look at the context of a verse. Here, the verse is talking about how the Lord's hand must be in something for it to work properly. Could it also be that rising early and staying up late does less good if the Lord's hand isn't in it? Perhaps it's a possibility. In any case, it's important to remember that we should rely on the Lord. We shouldn't trust in our own abilities alone – the Lord must be at the heart of everything we do.

"So whatever you wish that others would do to you, do also to them, for this is the Law and the Prophets." – Matthew 7:12

Business that God approves of requires a firm understanding and grasp of ethics. Thankfully, Jesus simplified much of the whole topic of ethics in just a few words commonly known as the Golden Rule. As Real Estate Professionals, put yourselves into other people's shoes, you're more likely to treat those people as you'd like to be treated. Here are a few business questions you can use to do the best thing for your customers/clients:

If I was the customer/client, would I be happy with the speed of service of my business?

If I was the customer/client, would I appreciate how my business communicates with me?

If I was the customer/client, would I continue doing business with my business?

These questions can help you improve customer/client satisfaction.

The beginning of wisdom is this: "Get wisdom, and whatever you get, get insight." – Proverbs 4:7

I continually educate myself about all things Real Estate. I attend presentations and do a lot of research. Understanding is of great value in my business, and I've be willing to guess it is in yours too. Wisdom not only includes having knowledge and experience, but it also includes being able to use that knowledge and experience in a sound way – it involves proper judgment.

Notice the value of understanding: "Though it cost all you have, get understanding." That's right, understanding is worth everything you own. Now, you probably don't have to go and sell everything you own to take a course that costs thousands and thousands of dollars, but this verse certainly highlights the value of understanding. Make a sincere effort to always be a learner. Value education. Learn how to apply your knowledge in business and life. It's worth a lot.

"In all toil there is profit, but mere talk tends only to poverty." – Proverbs 14:23

In my experience, I've learned the reason why so many people don't make it is because they aren't really willing to put in the hard work required to succeed. They are all talk, no action.

You've probably heard that "actions speak louder than words." True. But many people think that means you must act and speak. What if you just did the right thing without announcing it to the world? One might argue that that could result in less accountability, but if you follow through on your goals without speaking, it will show a sense of humility coupled with a dedication to working hard.

Work hard, and you can overcome many business challenges.

"For what does it profit a man to gain the whole world and forfeit his soul?" – Mark 8:36

I have done quite well financially in my lifetime. I know others who are quite wealthy too. But let me tell you, the numbers don't mean a thing compared to the gift that my Lord Jesus gave to me on the cross. If you're not a Christian, I ask you to look into the life of Christ. Listen, we've all messed up. We've all fallen short of the perfection of God. We're sinners! But God loves us so much that he came down to this planet to rescue us from the spiritual consequences of our actions. His name is Jesus.

If you're a Real Estate Professional – or anyone else – who doesn't yet have a relationship with Christ, seek first God's kingdom. Wealth is deceitful, and it doesn't mean a thing compared to the glorious riches in Christ.

"The plans of the diligent lead surely to abundance, but everyone who is hasty comes only to poverty." – Proverbs 21:5

Diligence means showing care – many times over the long haul. Are you showing diligence?

Businesses must be carefully built. Don't be hasty. Remember that it can take years to see some success. If you go for a quick win, you might find yourself with a quick failure.

Now go make some money but put God first!

Bible Verses To Encourage You Along Your Real Estate Industry Journey.

Running your Real Estate Business is a spiritual journey as much as a road trip to business success. Along the road, you will be tested, stretched and stressed and these words from the bible will give you needed encouragement.

"For I know the plans I have for you," declares the Lord, "plans to prosper you and not to harm you, plans to give you hope and a future." - Jeremiah 29:11-13

Almighty Father, please make me believe in my ability to manifest dreams. Then you will call on me and come and pray to me, and I will listen to you. You will seek me and find me when you seek me with all your heart." In order to have a successful business, you must trust in the Lord. God's will is what is best for you. There will be times when you do not understand why things are happening in your business, but God is always trying to teach and to protect you.

"I consider that our present sufferings are not worth comparing with the glory that will be revealed in us." - Romans 8:18

I never sweat the small stuff and love what I do. There is a saying "You wouldn't know good days if it weren't for bad days. So, you need to thank God for bad days too." Often in business when we don't close a sale or get a contract that we invested a lot of time in, we take it personally. Start thinking about things in your business differently. When you don't get a contract, it's because it wasn't meant for you. In some cases, God might have been protecting you from a nightmare client.

He has filled them with skill to do all kinds of work as engravers, designers, embroiderers in blue, purple and scarlet yarn and fine linen, and weavers—all of them skilled workers and designers. - Exodus 35:35

Dear Father, please bless me with the will and the drive to succeed. God has given all of us talents that we can sell, but that doesn't mean you should start a business. Make yourself a student of business, first. Make sure there's a paying client for your product or service. Develop your business and leadership skills so that you can turn your talent into a real business.

"Take delight in the Lord, and he will give you the desires of your heart. Always remember who you are and who you are in Christ." - Psalm 37:4

I am rich because my inner resources are rich. We are not defined by our bank accounts or by how many plaques are on the wall. Never hesitate to share your testimony with others about what the Lord has done for you in business. God wants us to be fine examples of his light and love.

"Faith without works is dead." - James 2:26

I am successful because I have incredible faith and I know success lies with in me. You can't just pray for success. Develop a plan and work your plan. If you can do something about your situation, then do it. Stop making excuses, stop procrastinating, and do it*!*

"Behold, I am doing something new! It's already happening; don't you recognize it? I will clear a way in the desert. I will make rivers on dry land." - Isaiah 43:19

I make contacts easily and this creates great leads. Sometimes your business will need to move as the market pulls you in a different direction. You might need to reinvent your business, and you should not be afraid. God's always got your back.

Keep this Book of the Law always on your lips; meditate on it day and night, so that you may be careful to do everything written in it. Then you will be prosperous and successful. - Joshua 1:8

Today is the beginning of a new adventure as it is every day. The most important thing you can do for your business is pray daily. Start each day in meditation and prayer and you will stay calm as the day's struggles come upon you. Read words from the bible to stay encouraged and balanced.

"Commit to the Lord whatever you do, and he will establish your plans. Whenever you have doubt, go to the Lord in prayer and wait on God to give you the answer." - Proverbs 16:3

I am the best Real Estate Professional I know because of the support I receive from God. Remember that he speaks to us through visions and dreams, and sometimes he will send people who will speak his words to you.

I will give you hidden treasures, riches stored in secret places, so that you may know that I am the Lord, the God of Israel, who summons you by name. - Isaiah 45:3

The Creator blessed me with success as my birth-right and I will achieve it. Thought, determination and action eventually result in success. There is no such thing as luck, only blessings sent from God. When unexplainable things happen, do not be fooled that you did anything to make them happen. Always remember that God has already prepared a place for you to succeed and to learn.

"Our people must learn to devote themselves to doing what is good, in order to provide for urgent needs and not live unproductive lives." - Titus 3:14

I believe in my ideas and they repay me daily. God helps those who help themselves. If you do nothing, nothing will happen. Focus your activities each day on trying to accomplish 5 things before 11a.m. daily. You will feel less stress and get a lot more done each day.

As I think in my heart, so am I. - Proverbs 23:7

I am faithful, happy and contented in the work I do. Your thoughts can be your number one asset or your biggest liability. When you are alone in your office or back bedroom, your thoughts can easily turn on you. Your ability to stay positive, to learn from all experiences and to shake off mistakes quickly will be a big asset to you and your business.

"Commit your way to the Lord; trust in him and he will do this: He will make your righteous reward shine like the dawn, your vindication like the noonday sun." - Psalm 37:5-6

Help me do what no one else is willing to do, O Lord, for I aim to be successful.

There will be times in your life when no one will think that you are going in the right direction with your business. But no one can stop God's anointing. If he gave you the idea for your business, he will bless it. Stay faithful and focused. When you think you have no more to give, give some more and you will be rewarded.

Happy is the man who finds wisdom, and the man who gains understanding; - Proverbs 3:13 Through my faith, I am successful because I learn so much daily. You need to be a life-long learner in order to be successful in business. You should constantly seek to improve yourself and increase your knowledge about the business of running a business.

"Enlarge the place of your tent, stretch your tent curtains wide, do not hold back; lengthen your cords, strengthen your stakes. For you will spread out to the right and to the left; your descendants will dispossess nations and settle in their desolate cities." - Isaiah 54:2-3

Through the guidance of God, I see myself as a pioneer every day in life. You do not need to wait until you are rich and super successful to help others. You should help others now as you are building your business. That does not mean you should go hungry to help others, but do not be afraid to enlarge your tent to partner with "so called" competitors. There really is enough business for everyone.

"For I am convinced that neither death nor life, neither angels nor demons, neither the present nor the future, nor any powers, neither height nor depth, nor anything else in all creation, will be able to separate us from the love of God that is in Christ Jesus our Lord. No matter what you do, God loves you." - Romans 8:38-39

I am open to learning. He will forgive you. He believes in second chances and hundreds more if you need them. Be quick to forgive and to pray for a forgiving spirit. How would your life change if you loved unconditionally?

"But these things I plan won't happen right away. Slowly, steadily, surely, the time approaches when the vision will be fulfilled. If it seems slow, do not despair, for these things will surely come to pass. Just be patient! They will not be overdue a single day." - Habakkuk 2:3

I will always be successful thanks to my attitude. You need to understand that God's time is not your time. There may come a time in your business when you just know you have a contract, one that you really need and things fall through. Those are the times when you need to trust in the Lord the most. When you accept God's timing, you can learn to live in hope and enjoy your lives while God is working on your problems.

"But thanks be to God, who always leads us as captives in Christ's triumphal procession and uses us to spread the aroma of the knowledge of him everywhere." - 2 Corinthians 2:14

I will always be successful because I am a people person. Be thankful that you know God for all of his goodness. God wants us to be fine examples of his light and love.

"For I command you today to love the Lord your God, to walk in obedience to him, and to keep his commands, decrees and laws; then you will live and increase, and the Lord your God will bless you in the land you are entering to possess." - Deuteronomy 30:16

Jesus, because of you I know that people are grateful for the services I provide. When I walk in God's way, he blesses my business ventures just as he will bless yours.

"Trust in the Lord with all your heart. Lean not on your own understanding, in all your ways acknowledge him, and he will direct your path." - Proverbs 3:5-6

Learn something new every day. If you only lean on your own knowledge in your business, you will not be able to grow. You must grow to grow your business.

"Have I not commanded you? Be strong and courageous. Do not be terrified; do not be discouraged, for the LORD your God will be with you wherever you go." - Joshua 1:9

There will be contracts that you really need that you will not win. There will be days when you drop the ball on your customer service, but you cannot let that define you or your business. You will get another opportunity and even if you don't, God is with you always.

"God has not given me a spirit of fear, but of power, love and sound mind." - 2 Timothy 1:7

I am able to communicate well through the Lord. Making fear based decisions in your small business is never helpful. For that matter, making decisions in anger is not good either. Try hard not to be reactionary with clients, vendors or employees. Use factual information and up-to date financials to make sound business decisions.

Think about your Real Estate business. How can you customize your products and services to your clients? How can you make every client feel like the most valued client? It starts with doing to others what you would have them do to you.

Let Us Pray…

Father God: "even when I walk through the valley of the shadow of death, I will fear no evil because You are with me." Thank You, Lord, for Your perfect love, a love that casts out fear and gives strength and courage to meet the challenges of the world. When I am tired, give me strength. When I lose sight of Your purpose for my life, give me a passion for my daily responsibilities, and when I have completed my work, let all the honor and glory be yours. In Jesus Name Amen.

Position Yourself And Your Real Estate Business To Receive The Prosperity Of God

"Beloved, I pray that you may prosper in all things and be in health, just as your soul prospers."
– 3 John 2

With God on my side, I am easily able to make my living. I ask: "Lord, teach me how to prosper in my body and in my spirit, for then I am well equipped to receive your blessings over me and my business."

"This Book of the Law shall not depart from your mouth, but you shall meditate in it day and night, that you may observe to do according to all that is written in it. For then you will make your way prosperous, and then you will have good success." – Joshua 1:8

I have something valuable to offer those who work with me. I ask: "Lord, guide me to constantly keep your Word in my Spirit and on my lips. Show me what works best for me to stay in your Word and when or how to meditate on it."

"Therefore keep the words of this covenant, and do them, that you may prosper in all that you do."- Deuteronomy 29:9

I am rich in experience and wealth through Christ. I ask: "Holy Spirit, rise up in me the courage and the confidence to do what You tell me, when You tell me, and how You tell me to do it – whatever "it" is."

"'Now it shall come to pass, if you diligently obey the voice of the Lord your God, to observe carefully all His commandments which I command you today, that the Lord your God will set you high above all nations of the earth. 'The Lord will command the blessing on you in your storehouses and in all to which you set your hand, and He will bless you in the land which the Lord your God is giving you. And the Lord will grant you plenty of goods, in the fruit of your body, in the increase of your livestock, and in the produce of your ground, in the land of which the Lord swore to your fathers to give you.'" – Deuteronomy 28:1,8,11

I never look back but always toward a secure future. I ask: "Lord, keep my path straight. Correct me if I wander off course. Holy Spirit, bring to my remembrance all things you've already taught me. Help keep me to wholeheartedly commit to Your commands so that we are blessed in Your sight."

"And God is able to make all grace abound toward you, that you, always having all sufficiency in all things, may have an abundance for every good work." – 2 Corinthians 9:8

I am a powerhouse of information who helps others. I ask: "Lord, grant me everything I need to continue your good works as You direct me. May everything I do be led by your Spirit and magnified into never-ending good works to bring you all the glory and honor."

"The Lord was with Joseph, and he was a successful man; and he was in the house of his master the Egyptian. And his master saw that the Lord was with him and that the Lord made all he did to prosper in his hand". – Genesis 39:2-3

I believe in teamwork and am a great team leader. I ask: "Lord, let our success be a testimony of Your goodness and blessing. Encourage me to point to you as my great provider, to introduce them to you, and to offer to them the opportunity for you to become their great provider, too."

"Let them shout for joy and be glad, Who favor my righteous cause; And let them say continually, 'Let the Lord be magnified, Who has pleasure in the prosperity of His servant.'" – Psalm – 35:27

I am secure and happy and pass that security to others. I ask: "Lord, how I celebrate your joy in the prosperity you share with me and all those associated with Your business. I am humbled and forever grateful. May I always remember all prosperity comes through You.

LET US PRAY... Father God, when I trust in the things of this earth, I will be disappointed. But when I put my faith in You, I am secure. You are my rock and my shield. Upon Your firm foundation, I will build my life. When I am worried Lord, let me trust in You. You will love me and protect me, and You will share Your boundless grace today, tomorrow, and forever. In Jesus Name Amen.

SUCCESS Is On Its Way

Through scripture, we know that God wants us to succeed in life. By growing, using our faith and our trust in the Lord we can be strengthened to fulfill His will for our lives. This is true success.

"Success, success to you, and success to those who help you, for your God will help you." – 1 Chronicles 12:18

LET US PRAY...

We declare and decree that success is coming our way. As we patiently await You, Oh Heavenly King, we will praise You in the hallways.

We chose to step out boldly today in Faith knowing that the future holds the fruits of our success and all the hard work and dedication will multiply our effort.

We will look up to the heavens knowing that we made it when Your blessings start pouring down. In Jesus' mighty name, we pray. Amen!

We declare and decree that success is coming our way!

Here are some Bible verses to gain a better understanding of how God defines success, and how we can truly succeed in life.

*"Have I not commanded you? Be strong and courageous. Do not be terrified; do not be discouraged, for the LORD your God will be with you wherever you go." - Joshua 1:9

*"I can do all this through him who gives me strength." - Philippians 4:13

*"Take delight in the LORD, and he will give you the desires of your heart." - Psalm 37:4

*"The LORD was with Joseph so that he prospered, and he lived in the house of his Egyptian master. When his master saw that the LORD was with him and that the LORD gave him success in everything he did, Joseph found favor in his eyes and became his attendant. Potiphar put him in charge of his household, and he entrusted to his care everything he owned. From the time he put him in charge of his household and of all that he owned, the LORD blessed the household of the Egyptian because of Joseph. The blessing of the LORD was on everything Potiphar had, both in the house and in the field. So Potiphar left everything he had in Joseph's care; with Joseph in charge, he did not concern himself

with anything except the food he ate. Now Joseph was well-built and handsome." - Genesis 39: 2-6

***"Commit to the LORD whatever you do, and he will establish your plans." - Proverbs 16:3**

LET US PRAY...

Father God, let me priorities be your priorities. Your Word says that I am a partaker of the inheritance and treasures of heaven. You have delivered me out of the authority of darkness and transported me into the Kingdom of Your dear Son. Father, where Your Word is there is light and also understanding. Your Word does not return to You void but always accomplishes what it is sent to do. I am a joint-heir with Jesus and as Your son or daughter, I accept that the communication of my faith is effectual by the acknowledgement of every good work that is in me in Christ Jesus.

Father God, let your will by my will. I commit my works (the plans and cares of my business) to You, entrust them wholly to You. Since You are effectually at work in me, You cause my thoughts to become agreeable with Your will, so that my business plans shall be established and succeed. In the name of Jesus, I submit to every kind of wisdom, practical insight, and prudence which You have lavished upon me in accordance with the riches and generosity of Your gracious favor.

Father God, let your word be my guide, and keep me mindful that genuine success is a result, not of the world's approval, but your approval. I affirm that I obey Your Word by making an honest living with my own hands, so that I may be able to give to those in need. In Your strength and according to Your grace, I provide for myself and my own family. Thank You, Father God for making all grace, every favor and earthly blessing come to me in abundance that I, having all sufficiency, may abound to every good work.

Father God, Thank You for the ministering spirits that You have assigned to go forth to bring in consumers. Jesus said, "You are the light of the world." In His name, my light shall so shine before all men that they may see my good works glorifying You, my Heavenly Father.

Thank You for the grace to remain diligent in seeking knowledge and skill in areas where I am inexperienced. I ask You for wisdom and the ability to understand righteousness, justice, and fair dealing in every area and relationship. I affirm that I am faithful and committed to Your Word. My life and my business are founded upon its principles.

Father God, Thank You for the SUCCESS of my Real Estate business!

In Jesus Name Amen.

THANK YOU!

I want to sincerely Thank You for reading this book! But, the work isn't done here. Praying and applying God's Word must become a lifestyle in order to see changes. You must live God's truth… *"Therefore, get rid of all moral filth and the evil that is so prevalent and humbly accept the word planted in you, which can save you. Do not merely listen to the word, and so deceive yourselves. Do what it says. Anyone who listens to the word but does not do what it says is like someone who looks at his face in a mirror and, after looking at himself, goes away and immediately forgets what he looks like. But whoever looks intently into the perfect law that gives freedom, and continues in it—not forgetting what they have heard, but doing it—they will be blessed in what they do." James 1:21-25*

Through God's grace, he will give us the power to grow in him every day. Good God Bless You, Pastor Kanoee!

Made in the USA
Middletown, DE
09 April 2025